My Daddy Died and It's All God's Fault

S U E H O L D E N
—————— as told by Chris ——————

My Daddy Died and It's All God's Fault

Illustrations by Renée Graef

WORD PUBLISHING
Dallas·London·Vancouver·Melbourne

MY DADDY DIED AND IT'S ALL GOD'S FAULT

Library of Congress Cataloging-in-Publication Data:

Holden, Sue, 1950–
    My daddy died, and it's all God's fault / Sue Holden, as told by
  Chris : illustrated by Renée Graef.
        p.   cm.
    "Word kids!"
    Summary: The author recounts her nine-year-old son's grieving
  process following his father's death.
    ISBN 0-8499-0879-5
    1. Fathers—Death—Religious aspects—Christianity—Juvenile
  literature. 2. Parents—Death—Religious aspects—Christianity—
  Juvenile literature. 3. Bereavement in children—Religious
  aspects—Christianity—Juvenile literature. 4. Children and death—
  Religious aspects—Christianity—Juvenile literature. 5. Death—
  Religious aspects—Christianity—Juvenile literature. 6. Fathers
  and sons—Juvenile literature. [1. Death. 2. Fathers and sons.
  3. Christian life.] I. Holden, Chris. II. Graef, Renée. ill.
  III. Title.
  BV294.G84   1990
  248.8′6—dc20   90–23679
                                                        CIP
                                                        AC

Printed in the United States of America

1 2 3 4 9 LB 9 8 7 6 5 4 3 2 1

To Walt
Beloved husband, father, and friend

Contents

1 When Someone You Love Dies

My dad was terrific. He was my best friend. But he died, and it's all God's fault. When cancer got inside him, he got very sick and skinny. It made me sad to see him like that. But, I didn't cry. Instead, I started praying. I just knew God could stop cancer from killing him. God can do anything. All we needed was one measly little miracle. Was that too much to ask?

Even after Dad died I tried to make a trade. "God, if you bring Dad back, I'll do anything," I bargained.

I started with the most disgusting thing I could think of—the dinner dishes. Without being told, I'd head for the kitchen sink after dinner and start scrubbing.

What made this job so disgusting was my little brother's baby food. Pea-green and yellow mushed squash is gross.

I even cleaned my room. I made the bed, picked up my dirty clothes, dusted, and even vacuumed. For a whole week my room was spotless.

But, nothing happened. Dad was still dead.

Since being cleaner didn't work, I offered to trade places. God could have me instead. I stretched out on my bed, stared up at the ceiling, and waited.

I asked God to take me instead of Dad.

"Okay God," I said, "I'm ready . . . let's go."

I guess he didn't want me though because again nothing happened. I was still here and Dad was nowhere.

That's when I decided, God doesn't listen. I was through with talking or praying or anything else. I mean, if I couldn't depend on God why try?

The whole family was a mess. Mom cried constantly. Once she started, she couldn't stop. Heather, my older sister, was all sad and mopey, too. Even Matthew, the baby, seemed upset.

It was just plain awful. Sometimes I felt like I was going to explode.

Once I even decided that Mom must have given Dad the wrong medicine. She took care of Heather's asthma. And Heather always got better. So, why wasn't she more careful with Dad's cancer?

Well, it had to be somebody's fault. Dad wouldn't just die for no good reason. Then I blamed myself.

After all, I had pulled the fire alarm at school. I did it on purpose. And the whole school had to go outside. The principal, Mrs. Jaspert, said it was a terrible thing and I would have to be punished. But I never expected this.

If I had another chance I could make Dad better. I just knew I could.

Grown-ups tried to help. They'd say: "At last his suffering is over." Or, "He's happy now. . . . Your Dad's with God."

Well, I didn't want him to be with God. I wanted him here, with me.

When my father died, weird things happened. It might

3

sound crazy, but I had funny little daydreams. . . . I'd see Dad and me clear as anything walking through the park. It seemed so real . . . like we were really there . . . together.

He would put his arm on my shoulder real chummy like. Then he'd say I was the perfect height for an arm rest.

"Glad to help out," I griped.

"Hey, what's a son for?" He chuckled, like I should know this by now. After all I was nine years old.

"So Chris," he grinned. "Name two things you positively can't eat for breakfast?"

"I don't know. What?"

"Lunch and dinner!"

Dad's jokes were always so goofy! I tried not to laugh, but I couldn't help it.

Dad always got a kick out of those dumb jokes. He used to laugh so hard he had to hold his sides. He would start bobbing up and down and shaking all over.

The more he laughed, the more I laughed, too. It was a riot. I really felt silly, when I saw Bobby Spencer. He was one of my school buddies. But the strangers we saw made the whole thing funnier. They'd shake their heads as if we were a couple of dopes.

Sometimes I'd still be laughing when I would remember . . . "Oh yeah, Dad died. This isn't real."

Those daydreams made it hurt all over again.

I was all mixed-up. I'd get angry at nobody in particular. And I didn't know why.

Everyday I asked myself, "How could God let my Dad die? What will I do without him?"

Well, I finally got some answers. But it wasn't easy. Sometimes it got downright horrible!

4

2 Dad, My Best Friend

Dad was a champion boxer. He was big and strong and fun. A lot of people thought we looked alike. We both had blue eyes and blond hair.

He told me other fighters used to call him, "Candy Face Holden." That's because he looked sort of soft. But he wasn't. In the ring, Dad threw a pulverizing power punch. Then those fighters knew they'd been mistaken.

Dad told me all about his career in the ring. I was so proud I bragged about him to everybody.

Once he even bought me a pair of red boxing gloves. He said one day I might have to defend myself. I sure felt special wearing those gloves. "Boy, wait until my friends get a load of this," I thought.

Dad slipped his gloves on, too.

Then he knelt down and punched the air, waving me toward him. I swallowed hard.

"Okay Chris," he said, "give me your best shot."

Limply I tossed my arm in his direction. Dad swiftly blocked it, and I stumbled backwards. It didn't hurt. But I could tell this boxing stuff could get downright dangerous.

*Dad loved to box. He stuck out his chin
and told me to whack it.*

I told Dad I had had enough. Then I started taking off my gloves.

His eyes dimmed with disappointment. He sat back on his knees, resting his hands on his hips. "Don't quit," he frowned. "You really didn't try."

Deep down I knew he was right. But I was scared stiff. I knew zilch about boxing.

Dad figured out my problem. Then he showed me some punches. I was watching closely when the challenge came again. Dad stuck out his chin and told me to whack it.

Okay, I knew there was only one way out of this . . . I had to fight.

Taking a deep breath I heaved forward. My right glove somehow landed squarely on his nose.

With a loud thud Dad fell sideward and hit the ground.

Wow! For a minute I thought I had really knocked him out. Frozen in my spot, I wondered what to do next. Dad got up rubbing his sore nose. "That's more like it," he groaned.

He put his arm around my shoulder. Then he added, "Guess I won't have to worry about you." Dad seemed proud. He poured us each a cold drink. Then he started talking about our next bout. I didn't say anything. But I knew I would make any excuse not to do that again.

We had a lot of good times. Some of my best memories happened when I was little. Dad used to play monster games with Heather and me.

Each night, before we went to bed, he threw a sheet over his head and pretended to be a ghost.

Heather and I ran around the apartment screaming our heads off. Sometimes I'd get scared playing "Monster."

7

When that happened Dad would peek out from under the sheet and wink.

Yeah, those monster games were great, but they got awfully noisy. Once we hollered so loud the neighbors called the police.

When Dad explained the game, the police officer grinned.

"Just keep the noise down," he warned.

From then on, we tiptoed around, very quietly, until Dad caught us. Then we would bust out laughing. Mom said she liked the new game a whole lot better.

Of course, there were times I got plenty mad at Dad. Like when he taught me how to swim. Now that is a lesson I'll never forget.

When Dad was a kid, Pop Pop tossed him into a pond and said, "Swim back." Well, it worked. Guess that's why Dad decided to teach me the same way.

It happened the summer I was six. Our whole family went to visit Buzy and Gita May in Tuxedo Park. Pastor Charlebois was also there. I could hardly wait to go swimming.

I had never gone in the deep water before. So I was probably the oldest kid in the baby pool. But I didn't care.

I was minding my own business when Dad plopped into the water beside me. He had kind of an odd look in his eye. I should have known he was up to something. But I just ignored him and kept playing with my boats.

That's when it happened.

Dad grabbed me quickly from behind and forced me from the shallow side. I didn't want to go. I knew I wasn't going to like it.

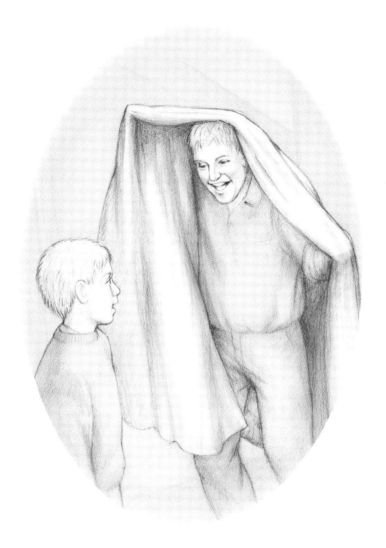

When Dad played Monster, we'd laugh and scream.

I guess I made the thing worse by grabbing his neck and holding on for dear life. I held on so tight I nearly choked him and drowned us both.

He tried to calm me down. He promised I wouldn't drown because he'd protect me. He said all he wanted to do was prove to me that I could swim. I just needed a little confidence, that was all.

All too soon we were in ten feet of water. We were bobbing up and down, water splashing everywhere. I knew I'd never get out of this alive.

Then he showed me how to swim by cupping my hands and reaching out. He told me to lean forward, kick, and let my arms and legs do the work.

"Do you understand?" he asked.

I kept nodding real fast, keeping my mouth shut. I was thinking if I just agreed, we could go back to the baby pool. Back to where it was safe.

But, Dad had other ideas.

He gave me a shove and hollered, "Swim Chris, you can do it."

"I can't," I gulped, but I had no choice. I kicked my feet and moved my arms as hard as I could. Dad swam beside me. I was so scared. I didn't see how I could make it.

Finally my feet touched the bottom, and I could stand. Boy, was I mad. I was crying and yelling all at the same time. As I got out of the pool Dad came toward me. He was probably going to say, "Congratulations!" or something. He seemed so pleased with himself.

But that's when I let out my zinger.

"I hate you Dad. I wish you were dead!" I screamed so

loud everybody could hear. Even pastor Charlebois saw the whole thing. But I didn't care.

Much later I thought that wish must have killed Dad. I really didn't want him to die. I didn't really know what *dead* meant . . . not like I do now. "God, You should have known that!"

3

Dad Gets Sick . . .
I Get Worried

Dad's sickness was tricky. At first, it didn't seem so bad. He was just extra tired after work. Later his back hurt so bad he had to lie on the couch a lot.

When the sickness first started, I tried to help. I'd bring Dad a glass of juice. Or, get him the paper to read. I'd start his bath. Stuff like that. But then Dad stayed sick all the time.

I got fed up having to be real quiet. He was always sleeping, and it was a giant pain for everyone.

I complained, telling Mom it wasn't fair. Why did I have to be quiet all the time? Sick was no big deal. Besides Dad wouldn't mind a little noise.

Winter was the worst time. We three kids were stuck inside for days. Matthew and Heather kept messing up my stuff. And that really made me grouchy.

It was no use arguing though. We still had to be quiet.

It seemed like we were being punished because Dad was sick. I didn't understand. Mom kept telling me to leave him alone and let him rest. But, after six months in bed, just how much rest can a person take?

Once I tried to find out why Dad didn't get better. Mom went shopping with Heather and Matt, so I slipped into his bedroom to investigate.

Quietly, I knelt down beside his bed and watched him toss and turn. In his sleep he jerked an arm or twitched a leg, then rolled over. I didn't see how he could feel rested with that much exercise. He looked all sweaty. His hair was matted down and wet.

The whole room had a stuffy sick smell. How could Dad stand it? Even I felt smothered.

Finally, he woke up and saw me staring at him. I didn't say anything. I just watched him blink himself awake. When he finally smiled, I knew it was okay to talk.

So I asked, "Why are you sick all the time?" Yawning, Dad stretched. It must have hurt because each tiny movement made him wince.

"I don't know why I'm so sick," he answered sleepily. "Even the doctors aren't sure. But maybe an operation might help."

"What's an operation?" I asked.

Dad explained how surgeons cut people open and remove the sick parts. It sounded like it would hurt.

"Ugh! That's awful," I said.

"I'd have twelve of them if it would help," Dad sighed.

I was quiet for a moment, and he could tell something was wrong.

"What's on your mind?" he asked.

"Well, I was just wondering," I said scratching my head, "If they yank out parts of you, how are they going to keep everything inside from falling out?"

13

Dad sort of chuckled, "Leave it to you to think of something like that."

Then he moved over, real easy like. He was making room for me to lie down beside him. It had been a long time since Dad and I had talked.

I scooted in and rested my head on his chest. I could actually hear his heart beating. Thump . . . thump . . . thump.

"Do you remember the time you slipped and hurt your chin?" Dad whispered. Oh yeah, I remembered all right. The cut was deep and blood oozed everywhere. I needed stitches.

Dad rushed me to Dr. Sinclair's office. And the doctor used a gigantic needle and black thread. He said it wouldn't hurt . . . but I didn't believe him for a minute.

I was so scared I tried to get out of there. But Dad held me down with his whole body. It took all his strength to keep me from flying off that table.

As Dr. Sinclair stitched, Dad said scars make a face look tough. I figured that would be really neat.

When Dr. Sinclair finished, my skin was sewed good as new. Except I had some wirelike whiskers for a while. Pastor Charlebois even said I needed a shave.

Anyhow I got the picture. Nothing would fall out after Dad's operation because he'd get stitched up.

After our chat Dad looked tired. I told him I'd be back later. Maybe then we could visit some more. He nodded, and before I got to the bedroom door, he was snoozing again.

After my talk with Dad, I was positive everything would work out fine. But, I was wrong. Nothing was ever the same again.

Mom started doing some very strange things. Once, I saw her crying while she was doing the dishes. I had never seen her cry before. I asked what was wrong, but she didn't answer.

I thought maybe the dishes upset her, so I said I would do them. But Mom just bent over the kitchen counter and cried even harder. I didn't know what to do. So I backed off. Maybe she wanted to be left alone.

I was glad when Mom Mom and Pop Pop came to visit. I thought they would help Mom not worry so much. But after a while they got to be real sad, too.

I couldn't figure it out.

Then one night Mom and my grandparents were sitting at the dining table, whispering. Heather and I were playing checkers. Suddenly Heather overheard something they said. She stood up trembling, "Dad's going to die!"

Quickly, Pop Pop darted from his chair and ran over to her. He threw his arms around her, smothering her with hugs. "No, your Dad is not going to die. We won't let him," he said.

It took a moment for it all to sink in. My head was spinning as I looked around the room. Mom covered her face with both hands. And Mom Mom just stared out the window.

Was everybody crazy? Of course no one would let Dad die. It just wouldn't happen.

But something seemed to go haywire inside me. I heard a loud ringing in my ears and felt cold all over. I sat on the floor, not knowing what to do. Something must be really wrong, but nobody was telling me.

Later that night Heather knocked on my door and said

Heather heard that Dad was going to die.

16

she couldn't sleep. I was glad to see her. I told her to come in. I couldn't sleep either.

As she sat down on the edge of my bed, I asked if she knew what *dead* meant. Nobody I knew had ever died before.

Heather mentioned Sara Thompson's old cat. Her mother said Sadie went to heaven and would never come back. But Sara could always get a new kitten if she liked.

We wondered what we'd do if Dad died. Who would take care of us? I didn't want a new father.

Heather said we shouldn't worry because God wouldn't let that happen.

We tried to feel better, but it was no use. We were plenty scared.

4 We Learn Dad Has Cancer

Operations take forever because that's how long Dad was in the hospital. At least, it seemed that long.

On the day he was due home, I got busy putting "WELCOME HOME" signs on the walls. Heather, Matt, and I designed all kinds of whacky "get well" wishes on poster board.

Mine was a picture of Dad in a hospital bed with a dozen thermometers in his mouth. Heather drew Dad in a daisy patch. Matt, well he drew a bunch of swiggley lines he was proud of . . . whatever they were.

With Pop Pop's help, I blew up a batch of balloons. We strung them together with yarn and looped them around our apartment door. For a final touch, we hung blue and red streamers all over. I wanted Dad to know we were glad he was home.

Then the apartment buzzer rang. Joe, the doorman, announced that Dad was coming up. Heather and I had it all planned. When Dad opened the door, we'd shout "Welcome Home." It'd be like a surprise party.

Then the door opened. "There must be a mistake," I

thought. "This couldn't be my Dad. This man's face was ghostly white with dark circles under his eyes. He was much thinner than my Dad. And he could barely walk. No, this couldn't be my Dad." But I knew it was.

Dad liked all the signs we'd made. And he told us he loved us more than anything. I could tell it hurt him to move. But he stooped down to give us each a kiss.

Yeah, this was Dad all right. There's only one Dad like him in the whole world, and he belonged to us.

I watched Mom help him into bed. Then he called me over.

"Want to see my scar?" he winked. "It's a whopper."

"Oh yeah!" I answered. "Does it look like whiskers?"

Dad lifted his shirt, and I rushed over to get a closer look. But, I wished I hadn't. It was gross.

I wanted to turn away, but my eyes were glued to his chest.

A long, squiggly scar crossed his entire stomach. Stitches were covered with dried blood while huge staples held everything shut. He looked like Frankenstein all sewed together.

Suddenly my own stomach started churning. I swallowed hard. Dad must have known I was about to throw up. He covered up his chest and told me to get a drink of water. I nodded and left the room. But I heard Heather ask if they got the sick junk out.

"No," Mom said. "Dad has cancer. We need a miracle."

I splashed water all over my face. Then I took a few sips of water and turned off the faucet.

Now I could hear Dad saying, "Yes, cancer is serious . . . but don't worry . . . I'm going to beat it."

19

"Well, I don't know what cancer is," I thought. "But Dad can beat it. Dad can do anything."

The doctor said some medicine might help. He called it chemotherapy. When Dad first got the stuff, it made him even sicker than before. He barfed for days.

He kept apologizing like he did it on purpose. Poor Dad, I knew he couldn't help it.

Months later Dad's sickness was no better. I pretended everything was okay. But way down deep inside I knew it wasn't. The only time he ever left the apartment was to get his chemo shots. Dad wasn't the same anymore and neither were we.

I was tired of Dad being sick. It was driving me crazy. Maybe he knew how I felt because once he actually tried to walk me home from school.

One day after school, Dad was leaning against the door of my classroom. He looked awful. His hair was all patchy, and his skin was kind of yellow. He looked like some monster in the movies.

I hoped no one in my class recognized him. They'd probably say, "So this is your Dad . . . the guy who's a big shot fighter."

I tried to slip out without anybody seeing me. But, my best friend, Johnny Davis pointed toward the door and said, "Hey, Chris, isn't that your Dad?"

Naturally, everybody looked over in his direction. Then one of the girls freaked out. "It's Freddy Krueger," she shouted. "The guy in 'Nightmare on Elm Street'!"

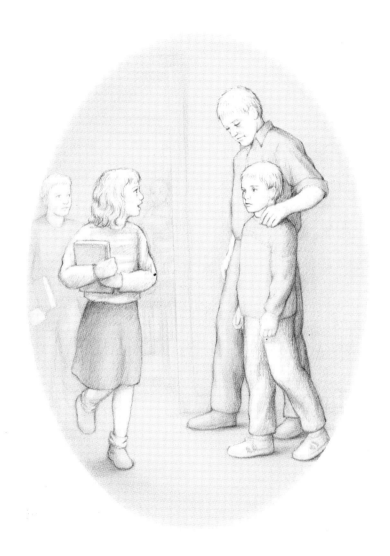

I was embarrassed when Dad showed up at school.

"That's not Freddy," Justin Finkel said, "It's Chris Holden's father."

Everyone got a charge out of that. They were all snickering as they went out the door.

I couldn't handle this anymore. It was one thing to be sick at home . . . but why did Dad bring it to school?

I wished he'd just stay in bed where he belonged. And I told him so on the way home. Dad looked sad and tired, and I was glad. He made everybody miserable. It was all his fault for getting sick in the first place.

When we got home, I slammed the door of my room and yelled, "I hate you."

Suddenly Dad came in and spanked me. At first I was surprised he had the strength. But after he did I was sort of glad. It seemed so . . . normal. And oh how I had missed normal things.

It's crazy, but after Dad died, I asked Mom who was going to spank us. Somehow it seemed important.

As Dad's sickness got worse, he would get all mixed up. Once Matt was sleeping in his crib, and Dad shouted, "Watch out, Matt's falling!"

When I explained that Matt was asleep, Dad just looked at me funny like. "Of course he's asleep," he said, "where else would he be?"

What really bothered me the most was when he didn't even know me. A few times he asked who I was and what I was doing here. It's weird when your own father doesn't know you.

Then one Saturday morning we couldn't take care of Dad anymore. He was rushed back to the hospital in a taxi.

There was no time for good-byes. Heather, Matt, and I just waved as Dad left.

Waving good-bye wasn't so bad. I knew I'd see him soon. Maybe next time, Dad might be a whole lot better.

But that never happened. Dad never came home again.

5 Dad Gets Worse

Monday morning everybody at school was excited. Our class had planned a Father's Day party, and all the parents were invited.

At the party each student was supposed to present special "Best Dad" awards. We worked for weeks painting cards and molding clay trophies. Mine was shaped like a boxing glove. I even hand-carved and lettered a sign. It read: "To Dad, The Greatest of All Time."

When class started Mrs. Hardy welcomed the parents and said we had something very special planned. Then she asked Bobby Spencer to stand up and start.

Bobby stood, faced his father and beamed, "You're the best Dad because you take me flying in your airplane." Then Bobby handed Mr. Spencer a blob of clay. Guess it was supposed to be an airplane, but it looked like it had probably crashed or something.

Next, Georgia Davis bashfully got up. "Dad this is because you buy me so many nice things," she blushed.

I had no idea what her trophy was. And I don't think her dad did either.

Justin Finkel jumped up next and tossed a clay ball toward his father . . . because they're Yankees fans. Mr. Finkel grinned and said it was the best trophy he'd ever gotten.

Next, Gina Peters made a big deal of presenting a goofy looking kite. To me it looked more like a pink rat with a long, lumpy tail.

While everybody else presented their trophies, I slouched back in my desk. All the other kids were anxious to raise their hands and have a turn. But not me. If only my Dad could have been there . . . but, he wasn't.

He was in the stupid hospital, and Mom was with him.

I looked down at the trophy I had made. I just wanted to squash it.

When everybody else had finished, it was my turn. I stood up looking down, but I didn't say a word.

Everyone just stared at me and waited. Then Mrs. Hardy walked over to my desk. In a kind, soft voice, she told me to sit down.

Like a robot, I did what she said because it didn't matter. I was completely numb . . . nothing mattered anymore.

After school I went home and trashed the trophy. Then I lay on my bed and stared at the ceiling. Not wanting to think about anything, I listened to the sound of my breathing. I took a deep breath in and a long exhale out. In . . . and out, . . . in . . . and out, . . . in . . . and out—it was a lousy way to live.

I couldn't sleep either. I had the notion that death was everywhere in our house. Maybe it was hiding in some closet or under my bed. I had to stay awake, so it wouldn't snatch me.

Besides when I slept I had nightmares. I'd wake up screaming. Zombies were everywhere in my dreams. They were creeping out of coffins . . . ready to grab me and pull me down.

I'd wake up in a daze. And I'd go through the whole day feeling really zonked.

One morning, over breakfast, I tried to act normal. As I poured a bowl of corn flakes, I asked Mom when Dad was coming home.

Even Mom seemed tired as she wiped off the gooey oatmeal smudged all over Matthew's face. Looking out the window she mumbled, "He won't be coming home." Then she just stopped talking.

I thought she forgot to add "SOON . . . he won't be coming home SOON." But with Mom I couldn't get a straight answer anymore.

Then, Matthew pushed his bowl of oatmeal away. He crumpled two cookie biscuits in his mouth and yelled, "Da Da, Da Da."

One Saturday morning not long after that, I got a lucky break.

No sooner had I stumbled out of bed than Mom said, "Want to go to the beach?"

Finally, something sounded fun. I remembered all the terrific times I'd had at the beach. Like, I used to bury Dad in the sand. Then he'd jump out, scoop me up, and together we'd crash the waves.

Anyhow, Mom said Mr. and Mrs. Reich were going and we were invited.

The Reich's are really nice people. Since they already

knew Dad was sick, we had nothing to explain. What a relief to leave all that behind.

Heather and I were so happy, we kind of danced around the room. Mom smiled and said, "Well, stop hopping and get ready."

Ten minutes later we were all set to go. We met the Reiches and their three kids at the garage.

"Chris, load the groceries in the jeep," Mr. Reich instructed. "Heather you take the blankets." Then Mrs. Reich strapped Matt and little Jackie in car seats. That done, we squeezed in next to Jody and Jeff. It was crowded, but no one minded. This was going to be a super day. Nothing could spoil it.

By mid-morning we arrived at Jones Beach. The air was hot and salty. Mr. Reich jumped out and hurried ahead of us. He wanted to find the best spot on the beach.

"Come on," he shouted, waving both arms. "This is it. . . ."

As we approached, we could tell Mr. Reich was very pleased with himself.

"Isn't this incredible!" he boasted. "What a great place for a sand castle contest!"

Then Mr. Reich picked up some sand and put it in my hand. "So Chris, what do you say?" he teased. "Want to take me on? Lilly will be the judge," he continued. "If I build the best castle, you owe us an hour's worth of babysitting. If you win, I'll grant one wish."

"I don't know," I mumbled.

"Come on," he urged. "What have you got to lose?"

"Well, okay," I said, still a little uncertain.

Mr. Reich knew my wish could never come true.

Soon I was busy building a fantastic sand castle. Even Mr. Reich was impressed. He said I won the contest hands down and I could have my wish.

So, I told him. I wished Dad would come home. As soon as I said it though, Mr. Reich's smile disappeared. Suddenly he was all choked up inside, and I didn't understand. Maybe I shouldn't have mentioned my father, but I couldn't help it. That was all I really wanted . . . for Dad to get better.

Mr. Reich put his hand on my shoulder and his voice got all trembly-like. He said if I ever needed him, well, all I had to do was call.

Of course, I thanked him and said everything was okay. I'd get my wish. Dad would come home good as new. He'd see. Mr. Reich wouldn't let go. Instead he pulled me closer and hugged me really tight.

From then on we built more sand castles and swam until we dropped. It was like Christmas in June. I wanted to remember everything so I could tell Dad. He'd be so jealous. That ought to make him hurry up and get better. I just knew it would help.

6 Dad Dies ... and I Can't Believe It

Our day at the beach lasted until midnight. That's when Heather, Matt, and I finally got home.

The sand had stuck to everything. It was inside our swimsuits, in our hair, shoes, towels . . . even our ears. And it itched like crazy.

Grandma Trautmann had flown in from Texas to keep Mom company. She made us a nice warm bath to soak in. And then we went straight to bed.

The next morning Heather had a bad sunburn. But we both were still excited about all the neat things we'd done. We had so much to tell Mom and Grandma Trautmann we could hardly sit still.

Heather told every detail about our beach adventures.

Both Mom and Grandma Trautmann were trying to listen, but they looked a little strange.

When the commotion settled down, Grandma whispered, "Sue, tell them what happened."

I was all set to hear how Dad was better and would be coming home. But, just as I sat down to hear the good news, Heather gasped, "Dad's dead, isn't he?"

Mom stared deep into our eyes. Then she swallowed hard, as tears puddled up in her eyes. Even though her voice was shaky, she managed to say, "Yes, he died last night."

I wasn't sure I heard correctly. Then Heather cried, "Oh no . . . not Daddy."

What? This wasn't happening . . . it couldn't be.

Somebody had made a stupid mistake or Mom was lying. Dad was all right. He couldn't be dead. He was just sleeping, that's all. I said I'd show them and started toward the door. I was going to the hospital to prove it.

Mom stopped me and took hold of my hand. Squeezing it, she said, "It's all true. I was with Dad when he died. . . . Dad's in heaven now with God."

"But, Dad can't be with God," I said. "He's supposed to be getting better. I wished it at the beach."

Running to my room, I locked the door. "This isn't real," I thought. "It's just some horrible dream. I'll wake up in a moment, and it'll be over. None of this ever happened. But, what if it's true? What would I do without Dad?"

Frantically I went rummaging through my drawer until I found a prized photo. It had been taken the day Dad surprised me with a new ten-speed bike. He was helping me mount it. The bike was too big and wobbly, but Dad was so happy.

At that moment I would have traded a zillion ten-speed bikes for him. Carefully tucking the photo back in my drawer, in the safe spot underneath the rock collection, I repeated what Mom had said, "Dad's in heaven now with God."

I couldn't believe it was true. If only I could take Mom back to the hospital, she'd realize Dad was okay.

Dad looked so happy in my favorite picture.

Mom was hugging Heather as I walked back into the living room. My sister was crying really hard.

Mom tried to explain how Dad had gotten a little weaker every day.

In a way I knew what she meant. Once, after school I called him at the hospital to say hello.

"Chris?" he asked, but then, he started babbling so badly I got upset.

Figuring I must have dialed the wrong number, I hung up.

Way down deep inside I always knew Dad's cancer was getting worse. Maybe God tried to warn me that Dad was dying. I don't know.

But I simply had to see Dad again. I needed to tell him how much I loved him. I needed to tell him I was sorry for ever hurting him. I'd make everything right again. I just needed one more chance, that was all.

"What were his last words?" I wondered as the news started to register. "Did he mention me?"

Mom said Dad wanted us to remember him when he was healthy . . . not like he was with the cancer.

As Mom spoke I didn't cry or anything. I just needed to see Dad again.

In fact, I made such a fuss, Mom finally gave in. She promised she'd take me to see his body. "But Dad won't look or feel the same" she warned.

Heather decided she didn't want to be left out and wanted to go, too. Mom asked if she was positively sure that's what she wanted. Heather said yes.

Neither one of us really knew what to expect. It was just something we had to do.

7 Dad's Never Coming Back

"Exactly what is a funeral home?" I wondered. I'd never seen one before. In fact, I never knew they existed.

On our way to Campbell's Funeral Home, Mom tried to describe it. "It's not really a home you live in," she explained. "It's more like a special meeting place."

"Is it scary?" Heather wanted to know, "Like a haunted house?"

"No," Mom answered patiently, "But, bodies are laid out in caskets. And it's where I made the burial arrangements."

I still imagined the funeral home would be sort of like visiting a haunted house, like on Halloween. But when the taxi pulled over to the curb, the place didn't seem unusual.

Built with red bricks and painted with a shiny white trim it looked real ordinary. Who'd have guessed a bunch of dead bodies were inside?

Mom paid the driver. Then reaching down she took hold of our hands, and made us face her.

"Are you sure, really sure, you want to go inside?" she asked.

I expected the funeral home to be like
a Halloween haunted house.

Mom was making us nervous. So, we simply nodded. We were too scared to speak. Then Mom walked toward the front door and opened it.

Inside the place was deserted. Out of nowhere a man appeared and asked if he could help us.

Mom explained who we were and why we'd come. The man quietly walked us to the elevator. He was nice enough and said if we needed anything to just let him know. Mom thanked him, and he left.

After that everything was deathly quiet. Even the elevator ride was eerie. Anyhow, Mom, Heather, and I were too choked up for conversation. I was expecting the worst.

When the elevator stopped on the third floor, my knees felt shaky and my mouth got dry as cotton. All of a sudden I wished we hadn't come.

I guess Heather felt the same way. She backed off toward the rear of the elevator. Her eyes pleaded with Mom for help.

"Honey, wait here," Mom offered, "You don't have to go."

But, Heather shook her head. No, she wasn't about to be left alone, not in a place like this.

Mom took our hands again, and we walked slowly down the hall.

In front of us was an open door. Beyond this door and in that room was Dad's dead body.

I wasn't so sure we were doing the right thing anymore. But I knew I'd never get another chance. I had to go in.

The room was huge. And flowers were everywhere. There were fancy sofas and chairs and coffee tables all done up like someone was planning a party.

By now Mom was crying again. She told Heather and me

how much she loved us and gave us a kiss. Her tears made my face all wet. I wanted to wipe them off with my shirt sleeve, but I let it go.

Then Mom combed our hair with her finger tips, like she used to when we were little. Guess she wanted us to look good for Dad.

Standing up she pointed us in his direction and whispered, "Say good-bye to your father."

Heather and I walked over to the open coffin. The lid was up and Dad was lying inside.

Yes, he looked like Dad, but different. His mouth was so still and stiff. I touched his hand. It was rock hard and clammy cold. I didn't understand. Dad never felt like that before.

Mom explained that his body had been injected with medicine to make it harden. This way, it would keep until he could be buried.

I watched Dad's face for a long time, hoping he'd open his eyes, and smile. He really didn't look the same. But, I was used to sudden changes in his appearance.

I also forgot all about the things I planned to tell him. Even if I'd remembered, it wouldn't have been the same.

Now I knew what *dead* meant, and I hated it. After it happens there's nothing left to say. It's too late already.

Then I got up close and kissed Dad's cheek. I wasn't ashamed. I loved my Dad.

"Chris," Mom whispered, "honey, it's time to go."

"Do you think he knows we're here?" I asked.

"Yes," Mom said. "He knows."

"Oh Dad," I thought, "why did you have to die and leave us all alone."

On the way out, Mom told us to remember Dad the way he used to be . . . strong, healthy, and full of life. I tried . . . but I couldn't.

Just as we were getting home, we saw our friend Mr. Jones. But he kind of looked away. It was like he avoided us on purpose.

"My dad died," I said looking straight at him.

Mr. Jones just froze for a moment and said, "Yeah, I know." Then he looked down just shaking his head. That was it.

I don't know what I expected him to say or do. But it called for more than just staring down at the ground.

I exploded.

"Don't you care," I shouted, "My dad is DEAD."

Mom told me to hush and come along. On the way up to our apartment, Mom explained that poor Mr. Jones didn't know what to say. Some people are afraid of saying the wrong thing, so they don't say anything.

Well, Mr. Jones is a grownup isn't he? How come he didn't know what to say. I thought grownups knew everything. Why couldn't somebody say something to make me feel better. But nobody would. Nobody could.

8

The Funeral

Three days after Dad died our whole apartment was packed with people. Everywhere little clusters of neighbors and relatives munched tiny sandwiches off paper plates. Even the hallways were jammed. There was no place to hide. I began to feel like I was in the way.

Besides, grownups always said the same old things. "It shouldn't have happened. Your dad was too young to die." Or, "Mom really needs you now. After all, you are the man of the house."

I wasn't ready to be a man yet. I was only nine years old. What was I supposed to do? Quit school and get a job or something.

If only Dad had told me how to handle this.

On the day of the funeral I wandered into his room looking for answers. Maybe he'd written instructions somewhere.

Wandering into Mom and Dad's bedroom, I noticed his rumpled up bed. Sheets were mussed with the bedspread draped half on the floor, just like when Dad used to be alive and sick.

Looking toward the door, I was all set to see him stumble back into bed.

Everything forgotten, I focused on the closed bathroom door. I just knew he'd come out wearing his grubby green bathrobe. Even though it had holes in the sleeves, it was Dad's favorite.

I waited . . . then remembered, "Oh yeah, Dad died."

I felt kind of like I'd been slugged in the stomach.

I walked toward his closet. So, this was all that was left of Dad—just a bunch of clothes.

Dazed, I looked around, trying to recall why I was standing in the middle of my parents closet. "Oh yeah, I was hunting for clues from Dad."

Slowly, I shoved suits and shirts aside. Then, finding his black leather bombardier jacket, I stopped. Taking it off the hanger I remembered something Dad had said.

"Stroke the fur collar and you'll have good luck."

Well, I rubbed that dumb old collar until it practically rubbed off. Still, I didn't feel so lucky.

I squatted down in the middle of the closet, hugging the jacket. Then I had an idea. Maybe, just maybe, God might let Dad come back. Well, it wouldn't hurt to ask.

"God," I prayed, "You can do anything. Please let Dad live again and I promise to be good. I'll never argue with Mom, and I'll do everything she says. I'll even clean up more. I promise . . . I really do."

After that prayer I felt a whole lot better. I knew God was listening and any moment Dad would appear. I laughed out loud imagining how happy we'd be. We'd say: "Wow! That was a close call." Dad would get a second chance, and this time we'd take better care of him.

I was in a whole other world with a healthy, happy family.

Seems like I was always going into some fantasy about Dad. This time the spell was broken when Mom called from another room.

"Chris, get ready for church," she said. "We can't be late for the funeral."

For the moment I ignored her. I wanted to stay put in case Dad showed up.

But Heather started crying, "Please French braid my hair. I can't go anywhere looking like this."

"There's no time," Mom answered. "You've got five minutes to get ready."

"Girls get silly about the dumbest things," I thought. "What's the big deal about hair, anyway."

Then Mom walked in and caught me scrunched in the middle of the closet. I must have looked kind of silly.

"What are you doing in the closet?" she asked.

Not wanting to spoil the surprise, I just shrugged. When Dad got back, she'd thank me for all I'd done.

"Hurry and get dressed," she said. "We can't fool around. People are waiting for us." Offering a hand she gently helped me up on my feet. Mom was trying to be strong, and I knew I shouldn't give her a hard time. So, just to make her happy, I got dressed.

A big limousine was parked in the driveway to take us to church. I'd never ridden in such a big car. Eight people sat in it, and we weren't even crowded.

When we arrived at the church, it was filled with people. The minister, Pastor Charlebois, met us at the door. He had been our friend a long time.

41

*Sitting in Dad's closet, I prayed for
God to bring him back.*

Bending down he shook my hand. "Hi, Chris," he said, "how ya doing?"

"I'm okay," I answered, trying to smile.

Actually, I was glad he cared, but he knew I was lying. He knew I felt horrible inside and nobody could change it. Nobody except Dad.

Next, we were ushered to the front pews. When we started up the aisle, I saw Dad's coffin. This time the lid was closed.

Imagine poor Dad tucked away inside, in the dark. He must be awfully scared in there. So, I begged Mom to open it, but she wouldn't. "The lid's sealed," she said, "no one can open it now."

Then everything was annoying. By the time the service started nobody knew how furious I was.

"My dear friends . . ." Pastor Charlebois was starting his sermon. But I couldn't listen. I kept thinking of a million different things.

Maybe God loved Dad more than me. Why else would I be left here without him. If God needed more people in heaven I'd be happy to trade places.

The others were crying now. But not me. After all we weren't supposed to be here.

I began to plot how I could lift the lid off the coffin. "It'd be simple," I thought. "Just tug the cloth, open the top, and spring Dad loose."

I was just about to do it when Mom took hold of my hand.

When the service ended everybody hugged Mom and said good-bye. I sort of shuffled my feet, stuffing both hands in my pants pockets. For all anybody cared I was invisible.

Later I overheard Mom talking to Pastor Charlebois.

"I'm worried about Chris," she said. "He doesn't believe Walt's really dead. He can't cry. I don't know what to do. . . ."

Well, I wanted Dad back. That's what I wanted to say. At least I was secretly doing something about it.

But I didn't say a word. Soon enough they'd find out why I didn't cry. I knew something they didn't. God and I had a deal and any moment Dad would come back. They'd see.

That evening Pastor Charlebois came to visit. He had come many times before to visit Dad. The two of them were best friends. But this time I knew Mom was behind it. So I pretended to watch television.

Pastor Charlebois asked me to sit down with him on the sofa.

I supposed we were going to talk about God. So I told him it was no use. God had no intention of bringing Dad back, no matter what I did. I didn't tell Pastor Charlebois that part . . . I simply said, "I'm mad at God."

"That's okay," Pastor Charlebois said. "God expects you to be angry. He gets blamed for everything anyway."

"Then why did He do it?" I shouted. "Why did He kill my father?"

"God didn't kill him," Pastor Charlebois answered. "Cancer did."

But what he said next surprised me even more. "You know, when I was thirteen my Dad died, too."

So, he really did know what I was going through. I guess I never thought other kids' parents died. At least none of my friends' parents ever died. I figured God was just picking on us.

44

"God doesn't pick on anybody," Pastor Charlebois explained. "Besides, we never really die. Life is just a trip we take before going to heaven. Some people just get there first."

Then I was curious. I wanted to know how Dad could be buried under ground and be with God at the same time.

"Only his body is buried," he pointed out. "His soul stays with God. Our soul is the important part that lives forever."

It was hard to picture Dad as part ghost and part skeleton. Just the thought of it made me laugh. Dad went through a lot of drastic changes. But imagining him as a bunch of bones struck me as funny.

When I asked Pastor Charlebois how he was so positive Dad was really in heaven, he sort of shrugged. "Because God likes to have good people around Him . . . that's why we were created."

That made sense. Naturally Dad was in heaven. He was the very best.

"Your dad's perfectly happy," Pastor Charlebois said, "But he'd be even happier if you were happy, too."

While lying in bed that night, I thought about all Pastor Charlebois had said. Yes, it was good to know Dad was all right. But still, I couldn't see why we couldn't all be together. I hated being left here without him. Once again, it seemed like it was all God's fault. I couldn't help it . . . it hurt.

9 A Long Talk with God

A few days after the funeral I was back at school. We had two long weeks left before summer vacation.

Mrs. Hardy acted a little strange. Whenever she looked at me her voice would get all choked-up. It seemed to be hard for her to even say my name.

The whole day she was extra nice to me. I didn't open a book or answer a single question all day.

"Hey Chris," Tommy Bellow teased. "How does it feel to be teacher's pet."

"I wouldn't know," I shot back.

"Well it's not fair," he complained.

"Ah, leave him alone," Bobby Spencer said, "Can't you see he's had enough."

Bobby's always been a good friend, and he was right. It was coming . . . I felt like I was going to explode.

It happened during lunch break. Gina Peters bounced off the swing and came toward the bench where I was sitting. Hoping she'd disappear, I pretended to read *Space Invaders*. But, Gina came right over and sat down beside me.

"How did your father die?" she asked.

"He had cancer," I said quickly, hoping she'd leave.

"Did you see him die?" she kept on.

"No," I snapped. "Anyhow, so what?"

"Well, I wouldn't know what to do without my daddy," Gina said. "I mean I'd just want to die if . . ."

"Shut up," I screamed holding my hands over my ears. "Just leave me alone!"

That was all I could stand. Jumping up I took off running. I bolted into the school building, down the hallway, and straight to the restroom. Shoving the door wide open, I nearly smashed the tiles behind it. Luckily nobody was there to bother me, so I locked the door. Then I really let loose punching the walls and hitting the towel dispenser.

I don't know how long this went on. But I was panting when I finally plopped down on the cement floor. It was coming. I couldn't hold it back. A wild gush of tears burst out. I was crying like I never cried before.

"Well God," I shouted shaking my fists toward heaven. "Are you happy now? I'm crying . . . Is this what you wanted?"

I ran my hands through my hair as tears poured out my eyes and down my face.

"You did this God," I shouted looking up, "So, you've got my dad. So what. I don't care what anybody says . . . You killed him. You could have stopped it. But you didn't. It's all your fault."

I was screaming loud. I didn't even hear someone pounding on the door and instructing someone else to get the keys.

I never knew it felt so good to cry. But, it was also draining. Suddenly I felt like a wet noodle.

47

That's when I noticed keys rattling at the door. People seemed to be speaking in muffled tones. Then Mrs. Jaspert was in the restroom. Some other teachers were there, too. I was so embarrassed. They all looked blurry through my tears.

Seeing me like this must have scared Mrs. Jaspert. She's the nervous type, anyway. Her head twitches whenever she gets upset. The first time I saw this happen, I thought maybe a bug had climbed inside her collar. But when somebody's head wobbles that much, it's got to be something more.

Even though I was a third grader Mrs. Jaspert talked to me like I was in kindergarten.

"Now, Chrisy," she said. "Everything will be all right. Come along, and we'll call your Mommy to take you home."

When Mom got there, my face was all red and blotchy from crying. She calmly walked over to the black leathered chair, knelt down, and held my hands in hers. Everything seemed okay as she stroked my cheek with the back of her hand.

"Let's go home," she said.

When we got home, I went straight to bed and fell asleep.

When I was asleep, I dreamed that Dad visited my room. He looked terrific wearing faded jeans with a blue V-neck sweater.

Wow, Dad's here! I jumped up and threw my arms around him. "Oh Dad," I cried. "It's been awful here without you."

Gently he laid me down and stroked my hair. We didn't speak, yet I understood. . . . He was taking care of me.

When I woke up, I remembered Dad's visit. Dazed, I sat up looking around, wondering where he'd gone. Just then Mom dropped by to check on me.

"Feeling better?" she asked. Then she sat down beside me, in the same exact place Dad had been, and we talked. I told her about what happened at school.

I even told her about my long talk with God.

Mom listened and said, "Look honey, it may take us a long time to feel better. We have to be patient and stick together."

Then I told her about my dream. I told her how I actually saw Dad and that he stayed with me awhile.

When I'd finished, Mom said something really neat.

"Your Dad will always watch out for you," she said. "When something goes wrong, Dad will march right over to God and ask Him to make it better. What other father can do that?"

Well, that made sense, but what about my long talk with God? After everything I had said, He probably hates me now.

"Don't worry about that," Mom said knowingly. "God doesn't hold a grudge. He loves you and knows how much you're hurting."

Well, if God wasn't mad at me, how could I stay mad at Him. I hoped Mom was right. I really wanted God and me to be friends again.

10 Our First Christmas Without Dad

Christmas came six months after Dad died. That was another hard time. I really missed him. Dad had always made Christmas special. He loved playing Santa Claus, and every year he went all out.

When Dad was around, Heather and I would wake up at the break of dawn. Then we would argue about who'd wake up the folks.

That last good Christmas with Dad, we decided to let Matthew do it. We carried him just inside the bedroom and ran back out to wait. When we figured he'd had ample time to do the dirty work, we took over.

Heather put on this big act—as if she didn't know what the baby was up to. Cracking the door open just enough to poke her head in, she said, "Matthew! . . . Are you in there?"

Matt was all smiles, sitting up in the middle of the bed screeching, "Da Da! Da Da! Ma Ma! Ma Ma!"

Mom and Dad didn't budge. They were still sound asleep. Well, this called for drastic action. We were desperate to get to all those presents.

I put Matt's Christmas present together . . .
Dad would have been proud.

Heather and I counted one . . . two . . . three then screamed, "Good morning!" That worked every time.

Mom and Dad moaned and groaned and tried to cover their heads with pillows.

"What time is it?" Mom asked, her voice sounding a little hoarse.

Heather checked her watch and answered, "5:32."

"Walt, you handle this," Mom said, trying to crawl back under the covers.

Dad groaned some more and said, "No one moves til I get some coffee." So, Heather, Matt, and I stayed by the Christmas tree, telling them to PA-LEEZZ hurry up.

Moments later Dad had his coffee. Then he blasted the radio on to the tune of "Jingle Bell Rock." Then he sort of shuffled toward the tree and lifted a present.

"Hmmm" he teased, "what do we have here?"

That meant, time to start.

Only one person at a time got to open a present, and Dad thought girls should go first. Since Heather was the only girl, besides Mom, she beamed. Everybody else had to sit back, wait and watch. The whole thing took hours, and we loved every moment.

So the first Christmas without Dad was kind of glum. We didn't wake up at dawn. We didn't even pester Mom. Once again we left it up to Matt. When he woke up, we started.

I remember turning the radio on, just like Dad used to do. Some guy was singing, "I'm dreaming of a white Christmas." So, what's the big deal about a bunch of snow. If I had something to dream about, it would be about Dad.

Mom did her best to play Santa, and we tried to be happy for Matt's sake. It was only his second Christmas. And he was totally thrilled with so many presents.

Mom kept the ritual of handing out one gift at a time. And each of us waited for a turn. But, it wasn't the same. Without Dad, the magic was gone.

I looked over at Dad's favorite brown chair. The one he called his throne. It was only an empty reminder of all we'd lost. Then tears stung my eyes. But thanks to Heather the sad spell was broken. She said, "Hey, remember the Christmas I got that incredible doll house. It looked like a mansion and Dad spent all day putting it together."

"Yeah," I remembered, "then it took him all night to assemble my gas station . . . we never did get the crazy sprinkler to work."

Suddenly Mom burst out laughing. I thought she'd gone bananas. She was laughing at Matthew. He was ripping into a big flat package. What was so funny?

Then I saw the picture on the box. It was a toy motorcycle. But it had to be put together. And there must have been a zillion parts inside that box.

"Guess I forgot about assembling things," Mom said, holding up five pages of directions. "We've got to put this monster together."

We fitted, glued, matched, and painted until we were completely zonked. Assembling things is a real pain.

Matt couldn't wait to ride it to the park. We were really proud as we watched him speed around sand boxes, swings, and slides. Maybe the motorcycle wasn't exactly perfect. The decals were slightly lopsided. But still, we knew Dad would've been proud.

I could almost hear him say, "Way to go. You did a great job." And knowing Dad, he'd probably add, "If only I'd known . . . you could have put that gas station together, too."

I kind of chuckled thinking about what I'd say, "Hey, what's a Dad for."

Oh, how I missed him that first Christmas. If only we could have had . . . just one more.

One Year Later . . . Getting Better

The first year without Dad was sort of lost. It took that long before I stopped looking for him. Guess I expected to see him just around some corner, waiting for me.

Once I actually thought I saw him. Mom was busy buying vegetables from a Chinese sidewalk stand when I noticed this tall, blond-haired man wearing a navy blue suit. His head was bent as he squeezed the lettuce.

When he turned his head, he looked directly at me and smiled. I was so disappointed I said, "You're not my father," and walked away.

I felt a lot like Ralph, my goldfish, that first year. I'd won him tossing ping pong balls into fishbowls at the school fair. I put Ralph in a glass fishbowl and placed him on the night table, beside my bed. Ralph was a pretty good goldfish, but he didn't do much. He just swam around in circles all day or floated to the top for air. Other than that, he was just there—all by himself, with nothing to do.

I was like Ralph for a whole year. After that I learned to adjust. But, I never learned to like it.

I really miss not having a Dad. Often I get the urge

to hang out with other fathers. I pay attention to what they do. Like if I spend the night with one of my friends, I'll ask their dad questions just to hear how they think. Sometimes I'll watch them shave or talk them into pitching baseballs. Most of the dads are really great about it. I guess they understand. For a few hours, I pretend they are mine.

At home I often wonder what Dad would've been like. Would he like to go camping or fishing? Or, would he be into basketball and hockey? Dad liked those sports so I guess I would, too.

It feels like Dad died a long, long time ago. Matthew doesn't remember him as much as I do. In fact, he doesn't remember him at all. He never really knew him. Sometimes he makes up stories to tell his friends. I know because I've been caught in the middle of them.

Once he told Stevie Easley that Dad was bigger than the Incredible Hulk. Stevie got scared because he was only a little kid. He pictured Dad as this huge, ugly, green monster.

But Matt wouldn't stop. He said, "Right Chris? Wasn't Dad as big as the Incredible Hulk?"

Well, I didn't want to embarrass Matt so I just agreed. "Yeah, Matt, sure he was."

Well, that did it, Stevie took off and never would come back to our apartment.

I don't mind when Matt makes up stories about Dad. It makes him feel like he really had one.

Even now I don't understand why Dad had to die, but I don't blame God anymore. It's like Pastor Charlebois said, "God didn't kill my father . . . cancer did."

The truth is, I never really hated God. I hated the sickness and the dying, but who wouldn't?

Sometimes I wonder how Dad felt about it. Was he afraid to die? I remember I used to be afraid of sleeping because maybe I'd never wake up.

One day, I decided to ask Pastor Charlebois about it. He was with Dad when he died, so he'd know.

On a beautiful fall afternoon, we walked through the park. Red, yellow, and brown maple leaves had scattered all over the ground. Occasionally I'd stoop, pick up a batch, and crunch them in my hand. When the wind gusted, all the tiny particles blew away. Then I'd pick up some more and start again.

I think Pastor Charlebois knew something was bothering me. Finally, I told him I was afraid of dying. And then I asked him if Dad was afraid, too.

Maybe I expected Pastor Charlebois to give me a simple "yes or no" answer, but I should have known better. Nothing is ever that simple.

"Chris, were you afraid to be born?" he asked.

Naturally, I couldn't remember. "What does that have to do with dying?" I asked.

Pastor Charlebois didn't answer right away. We stopped to rest on a park bench. Still quiet, he stretched out his legs and folded his arms across his chest. I did the same. "Was this how he and Dad had sat when they came to the park," I wondered?

Once we got comfortable, Pastor Charlebois continued. "Close your eyes," he told me, "and imagine a little baby before its birth." Then he went on to describe it.

He said, "See the baby's safely tucked inside this warm,

Pastor Charlebois said dying is a lot like being born.

cozy tummy. It's never hungry. It gets everything it needs or ever wants. Nothing can hurt it or frighten it. All it knows is goodness and gentleness."

It sounded so good I wished I could remember.

Then Pastor Charlebois continued. "But, that safe feeling doesn't last forever," he said. "The baby has to be born. All of a sudden things get topsy-turvey in his little home."

"Topsy-turvey?" I asked.

"Right, the baby's forced to come out and join the world," Pastor Charlebois said, "and nothing can stop it."

I opened my eyes, "Well maybe the baby isn't afraid because it's too little to know better."

Pastor Charlebois told me I was wrong. The baby is afraid because everything is startling. Before there was only a peaceful darkness. Now strong lights hurt his eyes. A doctor holds him upside down, and he's forced to breathe new air. Strangers touch and handle him. They seem so big. He's so very tiny.

Then a nice nurse puts him in a warm bath, gently washes him, and wraps him in a soft cuddly blanket. The baby probably likes her a lot. It's starting to feel safe again.

Then, the nurse hands the baby to his new parents. And they are glad to see him.

"The baby probably likes that part even better," I grinned.

Then Pastor Charlebois said, "Death is really like birth. Dying is leaving a familiar life behind. And like birth, it is just a new beginning. We're probably afraid at first . . . but once it's over, it's not so bad. Just different, that's all."

"Wow" I said, "I never connected dying with being born."

Pastor Charlebois said, "Death is just extra scary for people. We know someday we'll have to die," he said. "But the good news is we only have to do it once. Then we'll be home with God, our Father, forever."

He told me God takes care of his children because He's the perfect father. He loves us so much.

That meant God is really my Father, too. Well, I never knew I had two Dads.

Pastor Charlebois said that when we get to heaven we'll see everybody who got there first. They'll probably tell us we shouldn't have been so sad. They never really left us. They were just sort of hanging around heaven, waiting. Just like Dad is now.

A Letter to
the Reader

Dear Reader:

This book has found you because someone you love has either died or will die very soon. Maybe it was your father, too. Or, perhaps it's your mother, a sister or brother, a grandparent, an uncle or aunt, or a friend.

You'll miss them very much, and it hurts knowing they won't be close-by anymore. Somehow there's this huge empty spot in your life, and you just feel like screaming.

You're not alone. Others feel exactly the same way you do now.

Grieving is very natural, and it takes a long time before the pain goes away. You'll go through lots of different stages: worrying, being scared, feeling numb, feeling shocked, getting angry, and thinking nothing else could ever hurt so bad.

But someday the hurt will go away. Then you'll know how lucky you were to have loved someone so much . . . that you miss them when they're gone.

Before too long you will laugh and have fun again.

And remember, someday you will see the one you love

and miss so much. But for now they'll be waiting for you in heaven. They'll be watching out for you and loving you until the end of time . . . when we'll all be together again.

Until then God bless you,
Chris, Heather, Matt, & Mom

SUE HOLDEN is an award-winning freelance writer and author. Her previous book is *Saints for Kids by Kids*. She is the 1981 winner of the national Gabriel Award in recognition for excellence in spiritual writing for radio. She is a former senior copywriter for three major New York advertising agencies. Sue has a degree in journalism from the University of Texas. She and her three children live in San Antonio, Texas.

RENÉE GRAEF has illustrated more than a dozen children's books. Among them, from The American Girls Collection, are the Kirsten series and Paper Dolls. She lives in Milwaukee, Wisconsin.